I have got savings

    1. Stocks & Shares   -   Page 4

    2. Property   -   Page 9

    3. Premium Bonds   -   Page 15

Everybody

    4. Balance Transfers   -   Page 18

    5. Money Transfers   -   Page 24

    6. Online Sales   -   Page 28

    7. Current Accounts   -   Page 33

1. Stocks and Shares

<u>Risk</u>

This is by far the <u>most risky</u> investment product on the market. Only invest in stocks and shares if you are totally prepared to potentially lose most or all of your initial investment. Stocks and shares offer huge potential for growth; although likewise can lose their value quite easily in a short space of time! If an investment in stocks and shares is going to be considered you should put considerable effort into researching which stocks or industries to invest in first.

<u>Research</u>

There are many books which can be read regarding the different methods of investing in stocks and shares and different depths at which research can be put into investments. There are also different markets which can be invested in from different countries'. I chose FTSE which is the UK index although many people also invest in other countries shares and commodities. Unfortunately, I cannot offer any experiences in these fields as I have never reached into their potentials.

There are different accounts on the market, each with their own commission charges. You will want to review all of these potential accounts before deciding on which agent you choose to use to trade with. Most agents have their own merits, some being multiple trade discounts. Commission is reduced for these accounts depending on the number of

Epigraph

Have you ever finished work and thought "I should be earning more than this for what I do"?

Well guess what, now you can and without having to do very much at all! In some instances all you need to do is, well nothing. Yes that's right you don't have to put any effort in whatsoever. After your initial set up of some of the products & methods detailed below you can just sit back and watch the money roll in! If this sounds too good to be true it isn't; <u>**I have**</u> been using all of these techniques for many years now and they do work (some of them very well)!

There is no such thing as a (legal) get rich quick scheme and this book is not trying to tell you about them. There are some very naughty ways to make money but these are not those methods, and are all entirely legitimate and totally legal! I am simply making you aware that there <u>are</u> some very easy ways to supplement your income without having to do very much at all!

If you have got savings then there are additional methods you can use to more effectively generate profits with your money. If you don't have savings then there are still ways to make sure you can give yourself that little bit of extra cash when it's needed! It may sound like an old saying but, to an extent, it is true... "Money goes where money is"! Simply put, it's easier to grow your money the more you have. Even if you have got very little spare cash though, it doesn't mean you can't earn more very easily. The less you have the more you will appreciate this book as some of the methods are so simple you will wonder why you didn't think of them yourself.

I hope that the format I have presented this book in will make it easy to see exactly what to do and, under what circumstances to do them. <u>I am not a financial adviser</u> and am not in any way offering financial advice; merely sharing what I have done myself in the past to bring in that little bit of extra money every so often.

Check out the sections of this book on the next page and head straight over to the pages you want to read. I have tried to go into sufficient enough details but if you do want to know any more information simply send me a message or drop me a review and I will elaborate further where possible.

In these seven little chapters there is some very useful information which could potentially generate some huge sums of profits in your back pocket! Just give them a read and see how much difference they make to your finances; I know I enjoyed the extra cash!

trades per month/ quarter and is generally best suited to people with lots of cash to invest over several stocks. Other accounts have lower commission on average which may remain constant regardless of the amount of trades. This is clearly better for smaller investors. Reviewing the charges for dividends, scrip and DRIP schemes may also be something you will need to consider.

Practical Uses

It is my understanding that many pension funds will invest in stocks and shares in the initial years of investment. This gives the greatest potential for growth as any profits can be re- invested to create further income and therefore more profits. As the pension draws closer to maturity the fund will generally be switched from stocks and shares to gilt edged securities, property investment and cash accounts. This offers more security for the individual whose pension is being invested so as not to drop its' value by too significant a sum in the latter years before retirement.

Method

Not a great deal of capital is necessarily required for this type of investment but the larger your investment the smaller increase will be required to break even. This is due to a fixed fee being charged for commission in addition to a percentage of your purchase.

Worked example:

- Commission is £30.00 to buy (and sell) shares once

- This is 30% of a £100.00 purchase

Or

- This is 3% of a £1,000.00 purchase

To break even under each of these investments it is therefore necessary for the market to fluctuate by 30% or 3% before any profit is made at all!

For this reason you will need to find the best investment value to balance potential losses/ gains for your circumstances and level of risk.

My story

My personal choice of investing was to build a spreadsheet with many of the FTSE 100 companies' on it. This included their dividend payment rates and dates which assisted me in choosing the investment in the first instance. When I was ready to invest I would then update the current price per share using Macro's to quickly find the share price. If, based on the previous dividend, a high yielding stock caught my eye I would simply update the details with the most recent dividend rate and date. If a share goes ex- dividend for 2% in the following month this indicated to me that the stock was effectively 2% cheaper at that time. Whilst shares generally change in value closer to the ex- dividend date to counter the dividend being paid, I have found that this is not until much closer to the ex-dividend date.

Clearly this method of investment will have its' flaws as it is very focussed on the company continuing to pay a dividend and maintaining, or increasing, its' share price. Background research should also be conducted to ascertain whether the company is likely to suspend any dividend payments, or even if major changes are imminent within the industry. If something is likely to influence a share price then the stock possibly carries a larger risk and you may wish to look at higher returns if you go ahead with it.

My general thinking is that most shares pay higher than interest- yielding bank accounts and it is for everybody to assess whether they wish to indulge in the increased risk of investing in stocks and shares or not. If the risk is too much for you then please see my other investment options.

When it comes to selling shares, rather than trying to ascertain whether they are likely to increase further, I chose to give my investments a trigger percentage. This meant that no matter what is happening in the market, if my stock reaches 10% profit, it would be sold the very next working day. A stop loss was also chosen for these shares to prevent any unrecoverable loss in my investment.

In my experience, stocks and shares can fluctuate quite rapidly each day. This can be (but is not limited to) as much as 2% variation per day if nothing specific is happening in the market. Whilst not limited to this level of fluctuation, if there is something significant happening in the industry these percentage variations can be much higher, in either direction.

Included within any potential FTSE 100 investments you may be considering there are also "blue chip" shares. These companies are the larger multi- national companies whose shares are deemed "less risky" than other companies'. Share prices in these companies' should, in theory, fluctuate much less which in turn should make your capital investment "safer"! The flip- side to this is that your investment may not grow as quickly as if invested elsewhere and you will probably not make any large sums of money from investing in them.

I chose to spread my investments across "blue chip" shares and other shares. This, in theory, meant that whilst my investment should have been safer I potentially was profiting less than full investment in more volatile shares. My shares portfolio however was more balanced, which I understand to be a good thing most of the time as a crash in the market would need to be more widespread to impact the value.

2. Property

Risk

Investment in rental property is deemed to be much <u>less risky</u> than investing in stocks and shares. This type of investment can be done with or without any major capital to invest with.

Investment in property is usually a lot safer than other forms of investment, as the property market will not fluctuate nearly as much as the stock market under normal conditions. As mentioned in the stocks and shares section of this book, commodities will generally not fluctuate much either although there are obviously situations which may occur to fluctuate both of these quite significantly; influencing any investments with them.

The earlier an investment in property is made the less likely, in my opinion; you are to require the money imminently. Just make sure that you do not jeopardise any potential to purchase your own home if you choose to invest young. Whilst looking for your personal mortgage you may be offered a first time buyer mortgage rate which is generally lower than the standard rate. (Some lenders will discount that you have ever had a buy- to- let mortgage for this purpose; however many will class this as a first mortgage). It is; however, probably less likely that you will have the spare cash to invest in property at a young age. If a mortgage is required to fund your rental property you will need to consider whether the amount you are receiving less the amount you are paying is worthwhile:

Worked example:

- *Monthly mortgage interest £100.00*

- *Total monthly costs £220.00*

- *Monthly Rental Income £400.00*

The net monthly profit for this example is therefore £80.00 per month. You would then need to consider whether your net income of £960.00 is worthwhile (ie. Can you get higher returns elsewhere).If the amount invested in the property, for example, was £50,000.00 your annual profit percentage would be 1.92% p/a. If this example was genuine then you may certainly be looking to invest your cash elsewhere (if you could borrow the money at the same rate) to attain a higher rate of income than 1.92%.

Research

If you are looking to invest in property you should properly research the area in which you are considering and any potential charges which may apply. Other than that there is probably relatively little you can do to research where to purchase your property. It might be handy to have property nearby for ease in assisting your tenants although property in developing countries will probably hold higher rental returns.

The decision on which to choose clearly depends on your aversion to risk.

Method

The example mentioned in this section will only work if you persistently receive the same bills and rental income for the entire year. Residential tenants may tend to move around quite a bit and you may end up with periods of vacancy; meaning no rental income at all. Some of the bills for the property; however will still need to be paid (whilst your property is vacant you can apply to the local council for a reduction in council tax rates). It may therefore be important for you in these instances to consider fixed payment estate agent policies. This will give you a fixed, reduced, rate of income which you are guaranteed for a set timeframe. You may not earn what you might have with full rental income although you are guaranteed the money even if the property is vacant. You will need to consider your personal circumstances before agreeing to a contract like this. If rental income is your sole form of income then you may value this method of collections much more than if you have a salary supporting the property. If you have a supporting salary then you may choose to take a larger risk by just having rent when occupied, or even collecting your own rent!

Given that there is potentially poor return on investment, coupled with a risk to your capital, I feel that if you have a large amount of capital to invest this may not be your best option for returns. If like in the example above, however, you are planning on borrowing the money, with a mortgage for example, you are receiving a return on investment from cash you don't actually have at the time of investing! This is therefore effectively a loan with a negative interest rate (ie. You are being paid [by your tenant] to borrow the money).

If you are looking for a more reliable stream of rental income then you may wish to consider commercial lettings. Businesses will generally stay at sites for longer periods of time although any period of vacancy will also be longer. A mortgage for commercial property may also be harder to acquire due to having to evidence your business plan to a lender.

This form of investment may be the best way to build capital from nothing over time rather than having it to invest upfront. If you cannot guarantee being able to afford the repayments, however, you could end up having the property repossessed from you. I found that my salary helped supplement the funding of the mortgage interest.

This bit might be useful to people who have the money to buy property <u>outright</u>!

If you have the capital you may choose to leave your investment in a high interest; or other investment account. You can then monitor the interest rates to see if you could earn more than your mortgage rate is charging you. You will see the benefits of any difference in interest rates once the mortgage has been paid off. Just don't be tempted to take the money out of your high interest account for other things!

My story

When I was twenty-one years of age, I bought into my first property investment. Clearly investing in property requires your capital to be unavailable for several years'. As this investment was long- term; I was not expecting to need the funds any time soon. For added flexibility with this investment, however, I did invest with someone else. I therefore had the possibility, should I have required it, to withdraw some of my investment by selling par, or all, of my share of the profits.

At the time of taking out my buy- to- let mortgage it appeared that most, if not all, of the mortgages available were interest only. This clearly meant more freedom to repay the capital element of the debt. Although I received a fairly decent interest rate (attaining higher credit interest through my high interest savings account) it should always be considered whether to **repay** or **invest** elsewhere. This may make a small difference to what you profit by, but every little helps!

Worked example:

You have generated £10,000.00 in spare cash and wonder whether to repay the mortgage or invest elsewhere!

- *Your high interest account is currently paying 2.4% above base rate*

- *Your mortgage is currently tracking at a rate of 2.2% above base rate*

Given your £10,000.00 lump sum in this instance you should invest it in your high interest account. The difference is 0.2% meaning that over the year you will effectively receive this amount of your repayment in addition to your current gains. £20.00 won't seem like a lot over the year and you probably won't even notice it but it might buy you a meal out or some clothing.

3.   Premium Bonds

Risk

Premium bonds are a <u>very safe</u> form of investment which could, potentially, have massive payouts. One premium bond is valued at £1.00. They cannot be purchased individually, and must be purchased in multiples (currently £100.00). Premium bonds can be purchased directly from NS&I and will always be valued at £1.00 each. In addition to this they can also be purchased from The Post Office. Due to the bonds holding their value at £1.00 each you are guaranteed to receive exactly what you paid for them when you choose to sell. How can you make money on this you ask?

Method

Whilst you cannot make money on the value of your premium bonds themselves, prize draws are held every month for owners of the bonds. These prizes can range from £25.00 up to £1 million. Prizes are drawn every month so you may wish to be included in these draws by having some. For more information on premium bonds you can visit https://www.nsandi.com where more details are stored.

    The odds of winning a prize are relatively low meaning the chances of increasing your investment is also particularly slim. This being said, however, owning the bonds does mean that you do have the opportunity to win large amounts of cash <u>every month</u>! The only way you can lose money by buying premium bonds is inflation. In other words, £1.00 today won't buy you the same as £1.00 in twenty years time!

A minimum of £100.00 is required to invest in premium bonds so the amount of capital required is relatively small compared to other investments. This can mean that investing in premium bonds may be a desirable option to someone with little to invest. The more premium bonds you own the higher your chances of winning a prize; yet the higher your possibility of losing out at the rate of inflation also.

My personal opinion is that if you have a lot of cash to invest, don't invest it all in premium bonds. Invest a little amount by all means; but given the chances of winning a big cash prize are so low, most people are more likely to earn larger profits through other channels of investment.

My story

When I was a young child I had a small investment of premium bonds bought for myself and my sibling. On occasion, whilst I was growing up, my father would receive payments for winning prizes of our premium bonds.

Being young, these prizes felt much larger than they actually were and I thought it would be much better if I were to receive the full cash prize for winning (rather than half).

When I was just over the age of nineteen I therefore offered to purchase my siblings share of the premium bonds. Also being young they were more than happy to sell me their share for the cash. The value I hold is only small although I would not be looking to increase my investment any further at this time. This is because in the last twelve years I have not won a penny in prize money through this investment.

Going back to what I was saying earlier; although I haven't lost money on these bonds; I have definitely lost out on the value of inflation of the twelve years and any possible investment profits.

I will not be looking to sell my bonds any time soon as I certainly feel that for the level of risk my money is at, I still get the possibility of a very nice cheque appearing on my doorstep every month. Although not likely; I do like the possibility of waking up to the good news!

4.   Balance Transfers

Risk

Whilst not really an investment; this will help you to grow your money if used correctly. The only real risk posed here is that you will have to pay a percentage of the balance transferred. For this reason I would give this option a rating of low risk. You will definitely lose a small percentage during your switch although you will know what this is going to be when you move your money. So long as you keep up at least the minimum payment you should not be charged any more for moving your money. *The minimum payments will also slightly reduce your capital debt over the term (but probably not to zero).* Missing or being late for your payments will cause significant charges to be added to the debt and, on some accounts', they will also charge for interest on the entire balance (meaning big costs). If you have thought about moving your balance/s and are reading this book, however, you are quite likely to want to keep paying on time (by direct debit is best).

Method

You can move a balance from an existing credit or store card; paying a fixed rate of interest for the transfer! If you have built up a balance on store cards or credit cards and are planning on moving the balance to another credit card this can make you money! Firstly you need to consider whether:

- You will be paying a higher interest rate on your new card

- If you were going to pay it off in full, could you get a better rate of interest than the balance transfer rate

These are the two simplest questions you need to ask yourself; however there are other questions which you will possibly choose to investigate later on.

I understand that balance transfer offers are essentially designed so that you move your balance to a new company, paying them the interest rather than your old credit broker. You may receive offers in the post, by email or directly in person enquiring as to whether you want to do a balance transfer. When companies approach you to do this they may offer you quite attractive rates to move your debt to them. *The hope from the companies' point of view is that you take out the deal and continue to pay them the interest after the initial offer ends (but you are not going to do that)!* It is at this stage when you could seize the opportunity and make some money off of them by taking their offers!

Worked example:

You have a balance of £3,000.00 due on your credit card which is approaching the end of a beneficial rate!

a. You have got £3,000.00 available to pay off the balance and be done with it.

b.   You have no cash available to pay off the balance.

Answers:

a. If you are wondering whether to pay off the balance or re- invest you simply need to consider whether you will be paying more or less on your new rate than from your existing account. Depending on your aversion to risk it may be better to pay the balance transfer fee and invest you cash elsewhere (ie. If you are offered a rate of 4.5% for 18 months, you only need to earn around 3% p/a to break even with your costs). If your investments are in the riskier category; then it is quite probable that you will be able to earn more than this rate from your cash.

b. Under these circumstances you need to think about how long it will take you to repay the balance to your existing credit card company. The charges for credit cards are rather high so you could be paying 1.5% - 2.5% per month (around 18% - 30% p/a). You would need to look at the amount of interest you will be paying compared with the amount it would cost you to move the money (eg. If the monthly cost for interest is going to be 1.5% and a balance transfer is offering 4.5% for 18 months can you pay off the balance in three months. If the answer is no, then try and obtain a balance transfer to another credit card, paying the 4.5% upfront). Regardless of how long over the three months it may have taken for you to repay the balance, you are best setting up a direct debit to repay the balance over the term of your new card's promotional rate. If you don't pay off the card in full by the end of the promotional period you will have to make the same review again next year. If you want to keep your debt going and continue to make this review at the end of each term that is entirely possible also (and your total debt should decrease each time by a small amount too).

In both of these circumstances you should always make sure that you pay at least the minimum amount each month to avoid fees been added onto your balance other than the balance transfer fee. If possible you may wish to set up a direct debit to pay an amount of your choosing. This should help to avoid any further fees being charged on teh account for late/ non payment.

Research

If you are looking to make a balance transfer from one of your credit/ store cards always make sure you check your options. I find comparison websites are very good for comparing most of the options available; however I have noticed that banks do have offers not mentioned on these sites. Depending on how committed you are to saving money when making this decision I would suggest that you also check in branch at some of the banks before going ahead with a comparison websites results. Depending on your credit score and history, some individuals will not be eligible for the best rate balance transfer accounts; however if you have a clear history you will quite likely have more options available to you!

My story

When I was younger I built up a portfolio of shares whilst spending on my 0% purchases credit card. Whilst not spending any more than I would usually (this bit is important), I was not incurring any further costs at this stage and, instead, buying investments with the money I wasn't paying out (physically) for everyday products.

When the 0% rate on my credit card was due to expire, I chose to look around for a balance transfer promotional rate. This allowed me to keep my shares, which were paying dividends, and my debt was simply moved to another credit broker.

I continued this for several years switching between different deals when each one expired. My dividends (and share profits) were quite easily surpassing the amount I was paying for the balance transfers which is why I continued to move my balance every couple of years. This meant that for every year I extended my balance transfer promotional rate I was making additional profits on my initial spend. Over the term in which I was doing this; I believe I will have quite easily achieved profits of 50%; meaning everything I initially bought has effectively cost me half as much.

Was it not for wanting to start a family and obtain a mortgage etc. these profits could have continued for several more years; however I chose to repay the debt sooner to ensure I attained my mortgages and other necessary loans.

Given that this was money I was going to spend anyway (initially), any profits I have made from this method were generated entirely from nothing. The only minimal risk I had was that my alternative investment did not perform; although this could have been countered at any point by simply extending the 0% balance transfer further until it was (hopefully) back in profit. **Alternatively; I could have lowered my exposure to risk by placing the cash in lower risk investments!**

Whilst ever the initial capital investment was not performing; I was still being paid dividends at a higher rate than I was paying for the balance transfer. This therefore meant that, for as long as I continued to receive dividends, I could still make a profit.

5. Money Transfers

Risk

This type of investment, like balance transfers, is partly driven by your aversion to risk! This is due to any money you borrow having to be invested in something; of your risk choice. The risk category for this is therefore variable and almost entirely up to you. It is **_almost_** entirely due to the fact that you will still have a fixed cost element involved, which will vary depending on how good an initial deal you get!

Method

A money transfer rate may be offered at 0% for a set amount of time by you bank, building society or other credit broker. Whilst you can therefore be lent a balance of cash which you choose the amount of (to an extent) you will need a valid reason for the money to be lent. A lender will, for example, not lend you the money if you are planning to invest it elsewhere or reduce existing credit balances. Once the cash is given to you a percentage will be added to the balance, which will be your money transfer fee. The total of the borrowing will then be repayable. Depending on how long you take the money transfer over will depend on how long you choose to pay it back.

Worked example

You are offered a money transfer deal for 24 months at a rate of 6%. You choose to borrow £2,000.00 for a new car, (which you had already saved the money for). If your credit card provider agrees to your reasoning, they will add a balance of £120.00 to your newly given credit. If you set up a direct debit to pay off the total balance over the term of your agreement this will mean that you have paid 3% p/a more than you borrowed. However you wish to word it you will still need to make 6% over the two years to balance out your costs. If your approach to risk is something which makes you think this can be done then go ahead! All you have to lose is the 6% transfer fee (approx. 3% p/a), so you are fully aware of your exposure with this method. **Always remember that if you are repaying in equal amounts that you will only have half the total amount over the term to invest with!**

Research

As with balance transfers, not all offers are posted to comparison websites so make sure you check the bank branches too. Just remember that you should apportion the APR over the time of the offer. Therefore if you have offers of 24 & 36 months with fees of 4.0% & 4.5% respectively; the 36 month option will probably be better for you. This may not always be the case depending on your aversion to risk and how much you want to spend on your product/s.

My story

Just before the birth of my oldest son, my wife and I obviously needed to buy several items for the nursery. This was clearly going to be a large expense which would hit the bank account quite hard! Rather than purchase cheaper items which would quite possibly require replacing after a short while we decided to go with the original set we liked and my plan was to make investments to cover the gap in price.

Fortunately for us, there were several money transfer offers being offered around at the time; possibly owing to the recession! This meant that I acquired a very good deal on my balance transfer and was able to invest my saved cash elsewhere (in cheaper shares).

Before taking out the money transfer, I calculated exactly how much I could afford, based on my then current SIPP contributions. From there I simply cancelled my direct debit towards my SIPP for the duration of the repayments investing my cash elsewhere.

This money transfer therefore cost me only a small percentage of my original cash sum (which would not have been enough); and I used the cash I had saved to invest further in my SIPP (albeit all in one go).

The profit I made on my SIPP investment quite quickly surpassed my money transfer fee leaving me much more time to make further profits before the money transfer deal came to an end. I therefore made profit to the tune of at least three times my money transfer fee with little possibility of risk.

6.   Online Sales

Risk

If done correctly this method of profit making could cost you very little indeed; sometimes putting up no capital whatsoever. All it takes is a little time to set up your shop and you can be on your way. It may take up quite a lot of your time after the initial set up but could also bring in considerable profits. For the reasons above I would grade this method as <u>very low</u> risk.

Method

Setting up an online business in today's age is very simple indeed and you don't need any in- depth computer skills to do it! The method for this is very simple; set up an online shop and sell some items! The limits to what you can sell are seemingly endless; and if you wish to do this you should choose one of your favourite products; to retain interest. You will need to know how much you can buy the items for so that you know how much to charge (after commission) for each. You can sell almost anything which you can think of and each market will clearly have its' own merits, seasonal trends and drawbacks. By using a credit card you can purchase your stock after the order has been received from your customer, meaning you are almost definitely going to sell the item. You will need to identify the lead time for your items, taking into account any sourcing or posting time, and ensure you clearly highlight this to your customers'. The only way you could therefore not sell the item after you have ordered it is if the customer changes their mind whilst the order is being delivered and cancels the order.

If this happens, you do have an obligation under the distance selling act to cancel the order to your customer. Likewise, if you have purchased the items online, your supplier will also have the same obligation to provide you with a refund. Whilst they have an obligation to provide you with a refund (of all the cash you have paid to them) they are not obliged to pay for return postage. Therefore the only way you could potentially lose money from your order is if it has been shipped. To counteract this you may choose to keep the item at your address and list it as a "stock" item available for immediate dispatch to new customers. Returning the item will otherwise cost you the return postage which is not forced to be paid back to you by your supplier.

The above scenario is for if you choose to have the items delivered to you for dispatch; which may be the costlier option! The other option would be that you could have your suppliers deliver the packages directly to your customer. Many suppliers will offer a gift option; although you should probably be aware that they may advertise their business in the package they send out. This could influence your customer to look at the products your supplier is selling and ascertain how much profit you have made from them. If they do choose to do this they will probably not think about all your costs and therefore calculate that you have made a larger profit from them than you actually have. In addition to this, you will have no visibility of when or where the item is at any given time after postage. There is therefore also the possibility that your customer could claim for non- receipt.

Despite the fact that you may not have made nearly as much as your customer thinks, and you have put the effort into sourcing the product; this may provoke them to leave negative feedback on your sales site. This may have detrimental effects to your selling power, even if your products are plentiful and cheap!

I mentioned earlier that you do not need any significant computer knowledge to set up your sales site and this is true! Depending on what you are planning to sell online, there will probably already be a site which sells your items. Some of these sites, such as Amazon or eBay, will allow you to "piggy-back" off their site selling your own items. These sites will charge a small fee for the privilege of using their site and it may be cheaper to hire a website designer to set up your own site. The only issue with using your own website is generating traffic and awareness of your product; which unfortunately I cannot advise any further on (or I would be a millionaire)!

Research

The only research you will need to do for this method is finding out your suppliers and deciding on where to sell your product. If you can find a cheap supplier and the correct platform to sell your goods; you should be able to make some very handsome profits from this **trade**. After you have got your business up and running you will be able to think about possible methods to reduce costs and increase profit.

My story

Some years ago I was made redundant from my full time job and looking for work in my then current profession. This job search was quite difficult as the recession was prominent and not many employers were recruiting for my industry sector.

Rather than sitting back, claiming government allowances, and struggling to do anything worthwhile I decided to set up an online business. I was quite into video games & DVD's at the time and so decided to investigate how to sell these online.

After looking into this; it transpired that I could sell these items at a profit of between about 50p - £1.00 each (after commission charges). I therefore decided to list some items for sale on an online site, which I had purchased products from previously. I was aware that other users could sell the items for sale as I had previously purchased from one of these sellers myself.

Although the task would be quite huge to generate a catalogue large enough to bring in considerable profits; I now had some time to do it!

I therefore set to work investigating each item (by random word I thought of) and seeing how much I could purchase it for to make a profit when I sold it. At first I decided to set a target to list 50 items per day to rapidly increase my catalogue size and exposure to the market.

Before long I had built up quite a large catalogue of products with several different genres and interests. Doing this would spread my possibilities of making a sale over several different markets of consumers.

New games and DVD's fluctuate quite significantly after their release date therefore reviewing the prices on these more often, initially, kept my possibilities of selling the items open to the competition. **Clearly listing an item for £30.00 when somebody else is selling it for £7.20 is not going to generate much interest or many sales!**

After the first couple of months' I decided to lower the time I spent listing new items and spend more time looking for full time work. It still took quite a few more months' to find employment in the industry I wanted although in the time it took me to do so I had generated over a years' salary selling games and DVD's.

The only reason I stopped selling these items and went back to a full time role was that I needed a continuous stream of income to be able to apply for a mortgage. Online sales in video games and DVD's I found to be very seasonal; doing up to 80% more sales in November than October and well over 75% less in the summer months, whilst many people were on holiday!

7. Current Accounts

Risk

This is less of an investment and more of a common sense approach to being paid for nothing! If you have got a bank or building society account in the UK then you are eligible and in the current climate; there is <u>no risk</u> whatsoever to your capital (if you have any). You do not need any capital to generate cash in this manner and you will be 100% guaranteed to receive the cash if you comply with the individual rules!

Method

If you have a bank account with direct debits and a salary each month you will be able to qualify for income for absolutely nothing!

All you need to do is move your current account to another provider. Many providers offer different awards for switching to them and many of them can be found using comparison websites. It is not financially possible to make a bad decision when switching (assuming you get something) however there will be better offers depending on your personal circumstances:

Example

An individual with a regular £2,000.00 full- time salary each month and four different direct debits will quite *probably be offered better account privileges and awards than somebody with £500.00 variable part- time salary and one direct debit.*

Once you have found the account which is right for you; you can simply select it, enter your details, and the bank will do the rest. It's that simple; now that the "seven day switching guarantee" is in place you need do almost nothing at all after you have given your new provider your old account details. All you will need to do is provide confirmation to your new provider (and possibly your old one) that the direct debits and standing orders are correct. If they have missed any; simply set them up again with your new provider.

Research

As with balance and money transfers; not all available current accounts will show on all comparison sites. As I mentioned earlier; whilst switching and receiving a benefit can never be a bad thing (financially) there could be better decisions you could make to maximise your income here. You will need to put considerable research into how much you generally have in your account, how much you pay in and how many direct debits you have to maximise your income using this method. Even without much effort at all; you can still make a handsome profit here using very little effort!

My story

Ever since I held my first full bank account I have always enjoyed making money by doing nothing. For this reason I spent quite a few of my younger years searching the internet looking for better current accounts and places for my savings.

Loyalty doesn't seem to get you very far these days so staying with the same bank year after year for no particular reason, other than being loyal, didn't seem to make much sense to me! If I always bought my clothes from the same designer shop for example, just because, everybody would probably say I was mad!

Every time I have switched my account to another provider I have been paid by my bank (sometimes by the bank I was leaving too). Back when I started doing this it was nowhere near as simple as it is now. There were several forms to fill in before you would be able to have your transfer initiated and I believe that there were additional background checks done as well.

I am not sure what background checks are done now (I believe only if you need an overdraft) but I can't count how many times I have moved my current account. Sometimes this has been my main account where I had most of my bills taken from and sometimes it was where I kept my savings!

It didn't stop at one account either! Once I had moved my money about and was paying more by direct debits; I intimated that I could gain additional benefits by having multiple accounts with different banks. All I did was set up an account; and then switch some of the direct debits individually once the transfer had gone through. I was then free to open further accounts, switching and changing the direct debits to keep in line with the terms and conditions of my accounts'. Some accounts' simply said that deposits of £xx were required each month, not stating where from! This meant that I could set up a standing order going back and forward for a quarter of the monthly quota.

One of the accounts I opened stipulated that I must <u>pay in</u> £1,000.00 per month; although it didn't state where it must be from! I therefore set up a standing order from my high interest account to my new current account for £250.00 per week each Monday. This £250.00 was then transferred back the following day to my high interest account to minimise the loss of interest on my cash. Whilst setting up these standing orders was a little tedious (embarrassment meaning I went into branch on separate days to set each up) it did net me a small regular sum every month; which worked out at about 24% of my £250.00 lump sum each year.

Due to changes in the law and your banks temporary offers you will need to review the payments every so often (probably once a year) to ensure you are getting the best deals. Some accounts will simply offer cash for switching; therefore, whilst moving accounts every week is not a good idea, once or twice a year will probably bring some nice additional income in.

 Amazing Adventures @ shortstoriesforkids

Carl D. Nuttall

Audiobook titles available

www.ingramcontent.com/pod-product-compliance
Lightning Source LLC
Chambersburg PA
CBHW031514210526
45464CB00007B/2899